CONTENTS

INTRODUCTION

THE HOTTEST TREND IN temporary tattoos is jewelry-inspired tattoos, which can also go by the name metallic tattoos, flash tats, and shimmer tats. These silver and gold, shiny, glamorous, and completely wow-worthy ropes, stripes, flowers, geometric shapes, bands, and chains flatter and adorn the body, and are perfect for concerts, the beach, pool parties, festivals, and more. Celebrities and models love wearing metallic tattoos and have been known to showcase the body jewelry on runways and the red carpet. Now, you can join them!

Metallic tattoos come in a variety of designs and are a

creative way to express your individuality and style. From silver arm bands and rings to gold tribal art and necklaces, metallic tattoos can add a dash of glitz and a dose of sparkle to an otherwise ordinary look. They can be bold or delicate, romantic or edgy, over-the-top or simple. Whether you're looking for chunky arm bands to wear to a music festival, detailed body art for a trip to the beach, or one or two small pieces to add some simple sophistication to your next night out, the possibilities for mixing and matching these flashy tattoos are endless. We hope your new eye-catching ink makes you look brilliant and feel beautiful.

FUN FACT

One of the earliest metallic tattoos was created by self-proclaimed "Grandmother Flash" Miranda Burnet, and the trend has quickly soared in popularity around the globe.

STYLE INSPIRATION

YOUR KIT INCLUDES 12 sheets of metallic tattoos, adding up to more than 100 designs in total that can be worn as bracelets, rings, pendants, earrings, and body chains, or as decorative accessories and embellishments. The tattoos come in a variety of shapes like edgy arrows and geometrics, chevrons, lines, waves, swirls, and florals. Different designs suit different occasions and can be mixed with real jewelry or adhesive gems for an extra pop of sparkle.

Designs can stand alone for a delicate and understated look, or you can stack and layer your favorite designs for depth and complexity. Regardless of the look you choose, you'll be sure to turn heads!

Rings

Try placing some of the smaller bands around a few fingers or on your ring finger to act as a faux wedding or engagement band. You can also wear the ring above your knuckle, known as a midi ring. Try a stacked effect and layer a few bands on top of each other.

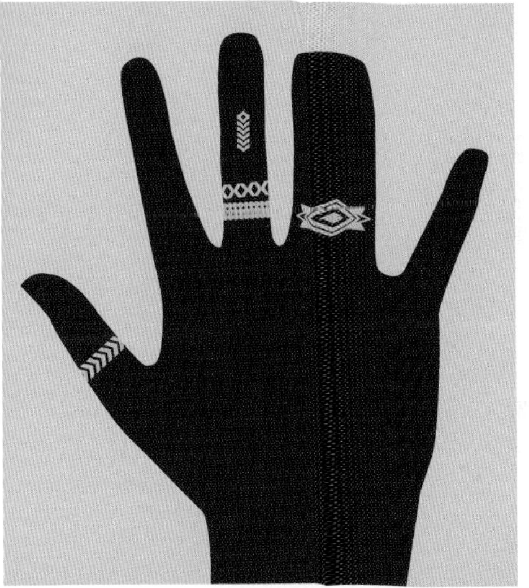

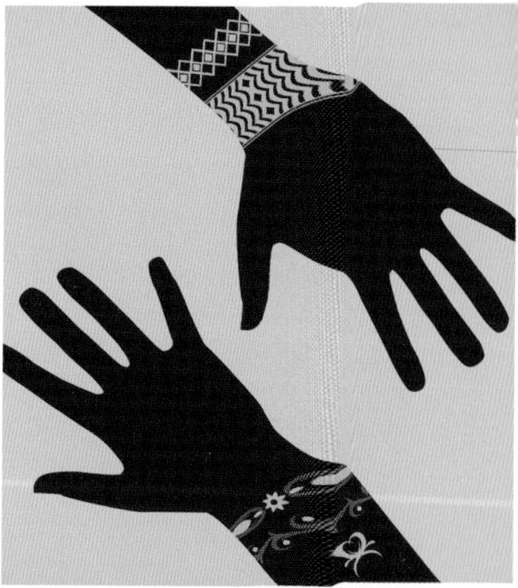

Bracelets

A small- to medium-length band can be placed on the top of your wrist and act as a cuff. Just like the rings, multiple bands can be stacked to create a layered look and/or combined with single embellishments like diamonds or starbursts for more variety. It's also fun to layer the metallic cuffs with real bangles.

Pendant

If you're looking for an alternative to wearing a necklace, the circular embellishments like the stars, flowers, and bursts can be placed on the upper part of the chest and act as a pendant. They can also be mixed with tinier tattoos for a larger more intricate piece.

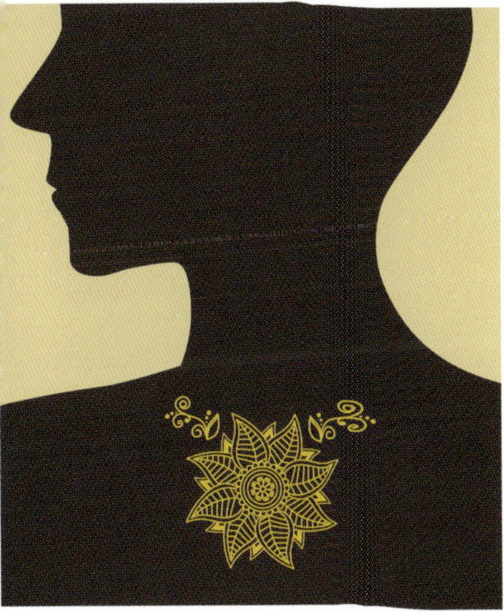

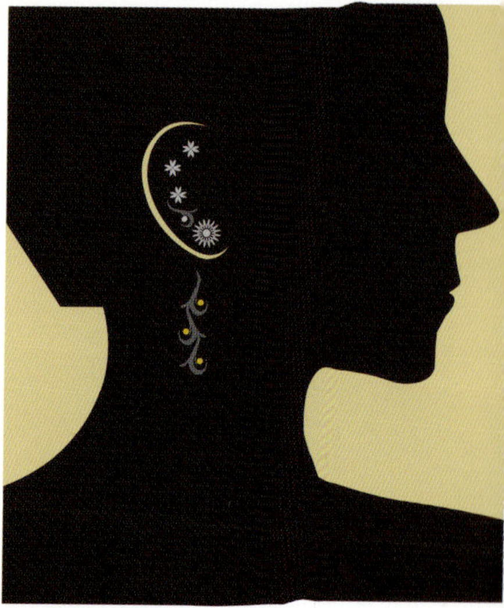

Earrings

Make yourself some tiny sparkly studs by cutting out small stars, diamonds, or bursts. You can wear just one simple design on each earlobe or play up the effect by lining the edge of your ear all the way up.

Other

Metallic tattoos can also be placed on other areas of the body including the upper or lower back, shoulder blades, upper or inner arms, back of neck, lower torso, ankle, or stomach. Just like the rings, bracelets, pendants, and earrings, the tattoos can be layered or stacked together for a more detailed design.

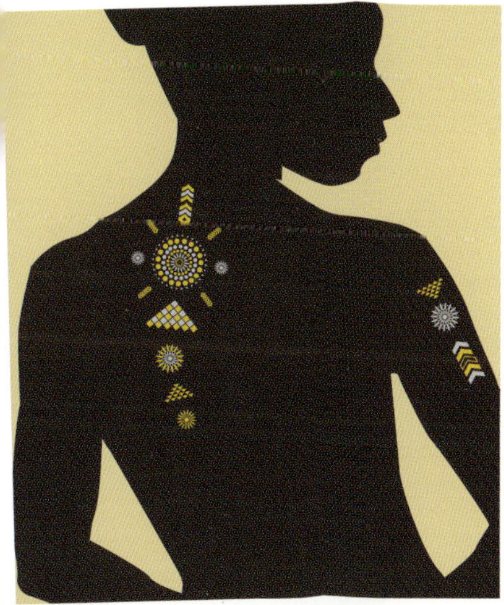

APPLICATION & REMOVAL

ONE OF THE ADVANTAGES of metallic tattoos is that when you're sick of a design, you can wash it off and start anew! Be careful and steady as you cut out the individual tattoo, and be sure to avoid ripping the page or cutting into other designs that you might want to try out later. Carefully position your design and apply it so that the transfer is made as cleanly and symmetrically as possible. While the designs are waterproof, it's recommended that you avoid putting the tattoo in direct contact with water, as the tattoo may start to wear off faster.

Application

1. Clean and dry the skin completely with warm water and a damp cloth before application.

2. Cut out the design of your choice and remove the transparent film.

3 Place the tattoo face down on your skin where you want your tattoo to appear.

4 Wet a sponge or cloth and press it firmly onto the back of the tattoo for at least 30 seconds to allow the tattoo to transfer to your skin.

5 Carefully peel a corner of the backing paper to check if the tattoo has transferred.

6 If the tattoo doesn't transfer, press the backing paper down again and re-wet with the sponge or cloth. Once the transfer is complete, any glue residue can be removed gently with warm water, if necessary.

NOTE: *Do not apply tattoos to sensitive or damaged skin, or near the eye area.*

Extending the Life of Your Tattoo

YOUR TATTOO CAN LAST up to five days if transferred carefully and cared for properly. Before applying the tattoo, be sure to use soap and water to thoroughly clean and exfoliate the area of skin where the tattoo will be applied. This will remove dead skin cells and other oils that might be lingering on your skin. For the longest wear, pick an area of skin that won't come in a lot of contact with oils, soap, lotions, water, or other elements. Tattoos on the hands will wear away fastest.

When the tattoo has been

transferred, you can apply a thin layer of clear nail polish or petroleum jelly, which will act as a sealant and help repel water. Try to avoid wearing clothes that will rub against the tattoo or create friction.

Removal

WHEN IT COMES TIME TO move on to another design, your tattoo can easily be removed with cold cream, baby oil, coconut oil, any oil-based makeup remover, spray-on sunscreen, or rubbing alcohol. To remove your tattoo, apply the rubbing alcohol or other removal agent to a cloth, cotton pad, or cotton ball and gently rub the tattoo until fully removed. Then remove the cold cream or oil gently with a clean cloth and warm water.

This book has been bound using
handcraft methods and Smyth-sewn
to ensure durability.

The dust jacket and interior were
designed by Susan Van Horn.

The text was written
by Jordana Tusman.

The text was edited
by Jessica Fromm.

The text was set in Futura,
Port Medium, and Nexa Rust.